No Name
CREEK

No Name
CREEK

Another Christmas Story

MARK GIBSON

Write and Release
PUBLISHING

www.writeandreleasepublishing.com

Twas long before these days of late, while
hiking 'neath December's moon,
A path beside a creekbed tried, between
the snows banked side to side, led on
to where thorned ivys twined.

And I, as always, in my unknowing, despite the hour, did trust to fate, and followed faintly snow etched trail. Alone, I thought each footstep fell.

The creek beside me, in its silence singing, with
bubbles and gurgles, and a rushing ringing.

Until at last, in utter silence, no more to think of,
to pray for, or ask, a pause in stride, and there
before me, in matching silence, in watchful
wait, a sphere of light shone in the night.

And there again was I to ponder, friend or foe?
My thought?
To run.

Yet stood there I, as if one frozen, upon
the path of this night chosen, instead
there knelt in light unknown.

And in the kneeling, light revealing, thoughts of friends, of family, and kin, of chances taken, of dreams forsaken, of life and living, came rushing in.

What else to do but pray for guidance.
Where else to turn, but to face the light...
To my great surprise, there was laughter, straight
from the heart, to think that after, all these years life
shared a secret, upon this night, within this thicket.

These days there's thanks for many things, for
sun and winds and rains, for sleeping sighs,
and family ties, for love, and loss, and gain,

for all the world might choose to
share just every now and then.

For one night spent on No Name Creek,
and the light that shone therein.

www.ingramcontent.com/pod-product-compliance
Lightning Source LLC
Chambersburg PA
CBHW040902120626
46551CB00001B/130